Ripley's SHARKS

AND OTHER SCARY SEA CREATURES

Believe It or Not!®

Ripley
PUBLISHING

a Jim Pattison Company

Written by Camilla de la Bedoyere
Consultants Barbara Taylor,
Joe Choromanski

PUBLISHING

Publisher Anne Marshall

Editorial Director Rebecca Miles
Project Editor Charlotte Howell
Picture Researchers Michelle Foster,
Charlotte Howell
Proofreader Lisa Regan
Indexer Hilary Bird

Art Director Sam South
Senior Designer Michelle Foster
Design Rocket Design (East Anglia) Ltd
Reprographics Juice Creative Ltd

www.ripleys.com/books

ISBN 978-1-60991-231-4 (USA)

10 9 8 7 6 5 4 3 2 1

Library of Congress Cataloging-in-Publication Data is available.

Printed in China
in January 2018
2nd Printing

CONTENTS

27

TWISTS

JAWS OF DEATH

DANGER IN THE DEEP SEAS

Is this a big grin that would welcome you in—or does this great white shark prefer juicy plump seals over swimmers? Find out on page 8.

WHAT'S INSIDE YOUR BOOK?

TWISTS

Greedy guts!

This fish, called a "great swallower" fish, was found in the Cayman Islands attempting this very large meal—it somehow ate a snake mackerel that was five times bigger than itself!

Everyone's scared of sharks, with their big mean mouths that are crammed with flesh-ripping teeth. But do these mighty sea beasts really deserve their reputation as monster marine killers?

Join us on an underwater journey into the exciting waters of the world's oceans. We reveal the truth behind the stories, the facts behind the fiction—and we will give you all the gory details of how sharks and other scary sea creatures really live their lives. Be prepared for some surprises —the oceans are home to some freaky, fast, and fabulous animals!

These books are about "Believe It or Not!"—amazing facts, feats, and things that make you go "Wow!"

This one-eyed albino shark is real! A Mexican fisherman found the rare baby cyclops shark by accident after cutting open a pregnant dusky shark in the Gulf of California, Mexico. It was one of nine babies, and the only one with one eye!

KEY FACTS

Read more unbelievable facts when you spot a Key Facts box.

Look out for the "Twist It" column on some pages. Twist the book to find out more amazing facts about scary sea creatures.

SCARY SURPRISE

NASTY STINGING THINGS

Hunting prey is tiring, dangerous work, so some animals take a more laid back approach. They have exploding stinging cells that they fire at their prey.

Chasing, catching, and killing—that's all exhausting. It's dangerous, too! So why not sit back and relax, wait until lunch swims by—then fire a deadly stinging arrow straight into its flesh. It's so simple, it makes you wonder why all sea animals don't have stingers!

Gas-filled sac keeps the colony near the sea's surface.

Each tentacle is one big polyp, over 30 feet long, with serious stinging cells.

Portuguese man o' war

This bizarre beast looks like one animal, but it is actually a colony, made up of smaller animals called polyps (say pol-ips). Some polyps pack a powerful sting to catch prey, but others are in charge of digesting food.

Nomura's jellyfish

This giant is one of the largest jellyfish in the world and when fully-grown can measure more than the height of an average man in diameter. These jellies have killed at least eight people in Japan in recent times, and in their masses have affected fishermen's livelihoods by poisoning their catch and covering it with slime!

TWIST IT!

STINGY STUFF

The tentacles of a box jellyfish can dangle down 10 feet into the water.

Portuguese men o' war trail curtains of tentacles into the sea and can gather in huge groups to create a deadly threat to any living thing.

Anemones and jellyfish have just one hole that does the job of both mouth and bottom—that's disgusting!

Some anemones have lived for more than 80 years and, as these animals do not age, they could live forever (as long as nothing squashes, or eats them!)

BIG WORD ALERT
COLONY

A group of animals of one kind that live close together.

Jellies

Jellyfish are not fish and they are not made of jelly! Their soft body is cup shaped and ringed with tentacles packed with stinging cells. Jellyfish can swim, but mostly drift with the currents. A fish swimming through the tentacles is stung and its lifeless body is moved toward the jellyfish's mouth.

Box jellyfish

The box jellyfish (above) is one of the deadliest of all animals. There are 15 long, dangling tentacles on each corner of its box-like body, or bell. The tentacles are covered in small stingers, each one delivering a tiny dose of venom that causes massive pain. A box jelly can kill a human in minutes.

Drop-dead gorgeous

Anemones are among the most beautiful of all sea animals, with their squidgy colorful body and tentacles that sway gently in the water. They use their tentacles to kill animals to eat, but they also sting hungry predators that come too close.

Venus flytrap?

This creature could be mistaken for a pretty Venus flytrap, but it is actually a deadly sea anemone that captures and stings prey with its tentacles.

Found a new word? Big Word Alert will explain it for you.

Turn over to find out why sharks and sea creatures are so scary...

FAST AND FURIOUS

WHY ARE SHARKS SCARY?

Dorsal fin
Fins help a shark to swim fast, and in the right direction.

Bendy bodies
Sharks have skeletons made of a bendy bone-like material called cartilage. Squish your nose and flap your ears—they are made of cartilage too.

The shortfin mako is the world's fastest shark. You wouldn't want to be chased by one of these hungry beasts—they can speed through the water at up to 50 mph, and even jump 20 feet out of the sea to catch animals!

Super sensor
This is called a lateral line. It can sense movements and chemicals in the water.

Swimtastic-body
A bullet-shaped body that is packed with muscles allows a shark to almost fly through water.

...AND OTHER SCARY SEA CREATURES

FASTEST SAILFISH
PAGE 11
This is one of the fastest animals on the planet, and the fastest in all the world's oceans.

MOST SURPRISING CUTTLEFISH
PAGE 38
Cuttlefish are able to change the look of their skin in a second, and hypnotize their prey by creating pulsing bands of color.

POISONOUS PUFFER FISH
PAGE 22
This fish avoids being eaten by filling up with water and turning into a large prickly ball. It contains enough poison to kill 30 humans.

UGLIEST VIPERFISH
PAGE 10
A fierce predator of the deep seas, viperfish can have teeth so big they don't fit inside its mouth!

If you had to design a perfect underwater killing machine what would it look like? Probably like a shark! There are few animals that inspire as much fear as sharks, but why do they have such a chilling reputation?

Sharks have been around for about 400 to 450 million years, so there must be some secret to their great success. Check out this shark's brilliant body to find some clues.

Gills
There are five to seven gill slits —sharks use them to breathe.

I can see you!
Sharks can see almost all around them, and some can even see color. In bright sunlight the dark layers inside the jelly-filled eyeballs work like sunglasses.

Great sense of smell
Water goes into the shark's nostrils and carries with it lots of useful smelly clues. A tiny drop of body fluid—such as blood—from another animal gets a shark very excited!

Armor plating
Shark skin is incredibly tough because it's made up of tiny teeth-like scales called denticles. They contain enamel, like your teeth.

CHECKLIST
- ✓ A fish
- ✓ Lives in the ocean
- ✓ Bendy skeleton
- ✓ Toothy skin
- ✓ Dorsal fin
- ✓ Powerful jaws with lots of teeth
- ✓ Hunts other animals to eat
- ✓ Great sense of smell

FASTEST EATER WARTY FROGFISH
PAGE 11
This fish uses a special spine on its head like a fishing rod, tempting smaller animals to come close—it then sucks its victim into its mouth in a flash.

MOST CLEVER DOLPHIN
PAGE 34
Dolphins are sleek swimmers with big brains. They chase schools of fish at top speeds of more than 18 mph, and track them with their super-sense of echolocation.

MOST GORGEOUS SEA SLUG
PAGE 23
Sea slugs are coated in gorgeous colors, frills, fringes, or tassels. They have no reason to hide because many of them are very poisonous.

DEADLIEST SEA SNAKE
PAGE 23
This striped sea snake is a sea krait, and is one of the deadliest reptiles on Earth. Sea snakes have lethal poison in their bite, but luckily they are ultra-shy, and stay away from people.

LEAN, MEAN, KILLING MACHINE

It's known as a great white, a man-eater, a white death, and a white pointer—but we call it the most incredible predator of the open oceans.

GREAT WHITE SHARK

Great whites use stealth and surprise to sneak up on their prey, and then speed up for the final attack. They have even been seen leaping out of the water to grab a snoozing seal on an ice floe.

Great whites are hot fish! Unlike most fish, they can keep their body warm, even in icy water.

NEAR MISS

Great white sharks don't always get it right. This 12-foot-long great white misjudged its attack on this seal, and it ended up perched on the end of its nose!

BIG WORD ALERT
HABITAT
The place where an animal lives.

Great whites have a big bite—about the same as a large saltwater crocodile.

Average human

Length: more than 21 feet— that's the same as one-and-a-half average-sized cars!

Habitat: coastal waters and open oceans

Found: in most oceans

Conservation status: rare

Ripley's Believe It or Not!®

Ron and Valerie Taylor from Australia were the first people to film great white sharks without the protection of a cage. They filmed the live underwater sequences of the shark for the 1975 film Jaws, and have dedicated their lives to protecting sharks.

Why are great whites so amazing?

They use some smart tactics for hunting:

▶ they are clever and plan their attacks

▶ they creep up on their prey, slowly and silently

▶ they can turn on the speed when it's time to attack

▶ they take a big bite, then leave their prey to bleed and weaken before returning for the kill

▶ they are strong enough to kill large animals, such as seals and dolphins

▶ they can live in warm, cool, or cold water

▶ and most importantly...

THEY HAVE LOTS OF REALLY, REALLY BIG, SHARP TEETH!

HOW TO FEAST LIKE A GREAT WHITE

DISH OF THE WEEK

You will need:
One plump day-dreaming seal

INSTRUCTIONS

★ Slam headfirst, at top speed, into the seal.

★ Raise snout, drop lower jaw.

★ Push upper jaw forward to reveal rows of large gleaming teeth.

★ Move lower jaw forward and up, to impale seal on lower teeth.

★ Close mouth and chomp away. Enjoy!

How deadly are great whites?

There is no doubt that seals and dolphins are in grave danger when there's a hungry great white nearby. These sharks are also responsible for one-third of all shark attacks on humans but, most of the time, humans escape an attack with their lives. We probably don't taste that good to a shark, and they may only bite to defend themselves, or because they mistake swimmers and surfers for seals.

FOUL FISH FILES

Fat, flat, fast, free-swimming, or floating—there are trillions of fish in the sea and most of them are hungry hunters.

Fish have some amazing ways to chase, catch, and eat their prey. If you were a fish, what type would you be?

MORAY EEL

Its skin may be pretty, but that face is ugly! Moray eels look like big-headed snakes and lurk in cracks in the rocks. They grab prey with a mouthful of deadly, sharp teeth.

FRIGHTFUL

WOLF FISH

This fish needs a huge head to house a mouthful of teeth that would put a bulldog to shame. In fact, this fish has been compared to a ferocious dog, because it can crunch big, shelled animals in half, and has even attacked people wading in shallow water!

FEROCIOUS

If you were a viperfish your teeth would be 12 inches long!

VIPERFISH

The deepsea viperfish lives where food is scarce, so it has a neat trick to keep its belly full. It can create light to entice swimming animals to come near, then it opens its mouth wide for a fang-tastic meal!

FANGED

HAGFISH

It looks like a giant worm, but don't be fooled. This is a fish to fear, with one of the most revolting lifestyles of any animal. A Pacific hagfish mostly munches dead animals, but it also happily swims into the mouth or bottom of a fish and eats it from the inside out. Eurgghhhh!

FIENDISH

Hagfish are covered in a gross, gloopy slime. When they get too slimy, the fish tie themselves in knots to remove the goo.

FROGFISH

There are few fish quite as weird as frogfish. They sit motionless on the seabed, covered in warty or "hairy" skin that helps them stay hidden. When an unsuspecting fish swims past, the frogfish snatches it in a lightning-quick movement that lasts just 1/6,000th of a second—that's one of the fastest movements in the animal world.

FURTIVE

SAILFISH

FAST

A sailfish is not just the fastest fish in the sea, it's one of the speediest creatures on the planet. It can chase prey at speeds of 68 mph. Compare that to a cheetah, which reaches top speeds of about 60 mph. The sailfish's speed is an awesome achievement because it is much harder to move through water than through air.

FEARSOME AND FREAKY

UGLY MUGS AND ODD-BODS

Think you know what sharks look like? Think again! Forget the sleek, smooth body shape of a great white and prepare yourself for a short shark-shock!

There are over 500 species, or types, of shark in the world. They all have a head, body and tail—but apart from that basic body plan there are some surprising differences.

The classic shark shape is a long, slender body with a pointed snout and crescent-shaped tail. It's a perfect shape for fast swimming in the open ocean, but not all sharks share that lifestyle. You can sometimes learn a lot about how an animal lives and hunts by looking closely at its body shape.

Horn shark

My strange snout is really good for sniffing and smelling food, such as sea urchins and shellfish. Some people say that when I search for food I look like a snuffling pig, and that's why I'm sometimes called a pigshark (though my real name is "horn shark").

I don't look like a pig... do I?

Ripley's
Believe It or Not!®

This one-eyed albino shark is real! A Mexican fisherman found the rare baby cyclops shark by accident after cutting open a pregnant dusky shark in the Gulf of California, Mexico. It was one of nine babies, and the only one with one eye!

Goblin shark

Anyone know a good orthodontist?

Scientists think my peculiar snout may help me find prey. I live in the deep, dark sea where it is hard to find fish to eat, but electrical sensors on my huge honker help me sense anything swimming nearby.

Who are you calling a sucker?

Nurse shark

My blunt snout is the perfect shape for feeding along coral reefs. I can get my mouth real close to crunchy snacks, such as crabs and lobsters, and I even gnaw on a bit of tasty coral from time to time. My top trick is to feed like a vacuum cleaner and suck in lots of water. With it comes lots of juicy fish!

Frilled shark

Do you like my lovely frilly gills and jaws? I have 25 "frills" in my mouth and each one is made up of five teeth, arranged in a pretty cluster. Each tooth has three long, pointy spikes. I live in the deep, deep ocean, so very few people have ever seen me. I can open my mouth wide enough to swallow a whole octopus.

Are you "frilled" to see me?

SCARY SURPRISE

NASTY STINGING THINGS

Hunting prey is tiring, dangerous work, so some animals take a more laid back approach. They have exploding stinging cells that they fire at their prey.

Chasing, catching, and killing—that's all exhausting. It's dangerous, too! So why not sit back and relax, wait until lunch swims by—then fire a deadly stinging arrow straight into its flesh. It's so simple, it makes you wonder why all sea animals don't have stingers!

Gas-filled sac keeps the colony near the sea's surface.

Each tentacle is one big polyp, over 30 feet long with serious stinging cells.

Portuguese man o' war

This bizarre beast looks like one animal, but it is actually a colony, made up of smaller animals called polyps (say pol-ips). Some polyps pack a powerful sting to catch prey, but others are in charge of digesting food.

Nomura's jellyfish

This giant is one of the largest jellyfish in the world and when fully-grown can measure more than the height of an average man in diameter. These jellies have killed at least eight people in Japan in recent times, and in their masses have affected fishermen's livelihoods by poisoning their catch and covering it with slime!

BIG WORD ALERT

COLONY

A group of animals of one kind that live close together.

Jellies

Jellyfish are not fish and they are not made of jelly! Their soft body is cup shaped and ringed with tentacles packed with stinging cells. Jellyfish can swim, but mostly drift with the currents. A fish swimming through the tentacles is stung and its lifeless body is moved toward the jellyfish's mouth.

Box jellyfish

The box jellyfish (above) is one of the deadliest of all animals. There are 15 long, dangling tentacles on each corner of its box-like body, or bell. The tentacles are covered in small stingers, each one delivering a tiny dose of venom that causes massive pain. A box jelly can kill a human in minutes.

Drop-dead gorgeous

Anemones are among the most beautiful of all sea animals, with their squidgy colorful body and tentacles that sway gently in the water. They use their tentacles to kill animals to eat, but they also sting hungry predators that come too close.

Venus flytrap?

This creature could be mistaken for a pretty Venus flytrap, but it is actually a deadly sea anemone that captures and stings prey with its tentacles.

SHARK ATTACK

HOW SHARKS HUNT

Sharks are carnivores, which means they need to eat animal flesh to survive. Like all of us, they require food to grow, move, breathe, and have young.

Hunting is a way of life for all sharks. They are the supreme hunters of the oceans, and can kill anything from fish and crabs to turtles and large mammals, such as seals and dolphins.

Sharks are successful predators because they have the body parts to find and catch food, and they are also very adaptable. There are sharks in all of the world's oceans, from shallow to deep water, from the icy cold northern seas to the warmest tropical bays.

SANDTIGER SHARK

Sandtiger sharks are able to move up and down in water in fast pursuit of prey —they manage it by gulping air (to go up), or burping (to go down)!

Aggressive attack

Every type of shark has varying behaviors to warn other creatures, and other sharks, that an attack is possible. These threat postures show the common positions of sharks when they are ready to attack.

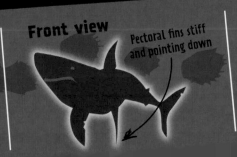

Side view
Snout raised, back arched

Front view
Pectoral fins stiff and pointing down

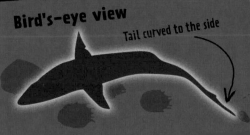

Bird's-eye view
Tail curved to the side

A twist in the tail

Most sharks attack with their mouth, but threshers use their enormous tail instead, catching their prey completely unaware. Threshers swim ahead of, or beside, shoals of fish then wallop them hard with their curved tail fin.

Now that's what I call a tail!

Big nose

Sawsharks have electric noses! Their long snout can detect the electrical signals produced by other animals. They also work like swords, because they are lined with long, sharp teeth. When sawsharks are hungry they sweep their "sword" until they find food. A quick swipe with their deadly nose blade, and it's all over.

KEY FACTS

ATTACK STATS

In the last 500 years, about 800 unprovoked shark attacks have occurred around the world (unprovoked attacks are ones where humans have not attacked or annoyed the shark on purpose). Which types of sharks carried out the most unprovoked attacks on humans?

Great white	33.4%
Tiger	12%
Bull	11%
Requiem	4%
Sandtiger	5%

Thirty other types of shark were responsible for the remaining 34.6% of attacks. Out of 800 attacks, 160 people have died.

Gang fight

Most sharks live alone, but oceanic whitetips prefer to stick together. They can be spotted in the open ocean in groups of eight to 200 sharks. Oceanic whitetips often follow boats, and will eat whatever they can find, making them one of the most dangerous sharks.

BOAT!

UNDERCOVER KILLERS

MASTERS OF DISGUISE

Cunning and camouflage are the tools of the trade for some marine predators. They take a smart approach to the art of hunting and stay hidden from view. It means they are invisible to their prey—and safe from attack by predators.

Smooth assassins are able to creep up on their victims, deliver a death-strike and disappear. The secret to success lies in the method, and these stealthy beasties know that a good disguise or hiding place is essential.

Secret snap!

Crocodiles may be famous for their ferocious attacks in rivers, but not many people know that some crocs hunt at sea, too. Saltwater crocs, with their darkly armored skin, lie motionless in the sea, near the shore, and blend into the rocky bottom—invisible to birds, fish, and turtles that pass overhead. The rock-like reptile bursts through the water to grab its prey with a single, quick snap with its giant jaws.

Scientists were surprised to see a coconut shell sprouting legs and running across the sand—a closer look revealed a veined octopus was hiding inside. The shell proved to be a great disguise for the soft-bodied predator.

Toadfish have thick, slimy skin and hide in dens near the shore, leaving safety only to hunt. It's a lonely life, so the males make loud burping noises to help the females come and find them.

TWIST IT!

Some sea creatures can change color to blend in with their surroundings, and engineers are copying the way they do it to build robots that can change color, too!

King ragworms are happy to swim in the sea, or wriggle along in the sand, but when they want to hide away they quickly burrow down, covering themselves with slippery slime. All that is left is a small hole in the sand—don't stick your finger in though, they have huge jaws and they bite!

The skinny trumpetfish disguises itself by swimming upright among coral and seaweed, and then sucks up animals into its large mouth. It also swims alongside big, beefy fish, protecting itself by disappearing into the other creature's shadow, and then strikes its prey when least expected!

Take cover!

Hermit crabs have a crafty way of creeping around looking for prey—hiding inside old seashells. They can quickly withdraw into the shell, and no one knows they are inside. Impressed? That's nothing. Cloak anemones then drape themselves over a hermit crab's hideaway, protecting it and throwing stinging tentacles at any predator that comes too close.

The anemone has pink spots and its tentacles are under the hermit crab, where it collects leftover scraps of the crab's meals.

Something fishy!

Imagine you are taking a walk by the sea, and you spot a strange rock on the sand—don't tread on that rock! It could be a stonefish, equipped with 13 large spines, each attached to two large venom glands that can deliver one of the world's most deadly toxins straight into your foot. Stonefish can survive for 24 hours out of water, so even if it looks dead, it may not be.

Meet the whale shark, the world's largest fish. Whale sharks are special sharks: they are gigantic, spotty, and serene. They swim powerfully, but at a slow steady pace, while sucking in water. Whale sharks can even hang beneath a school of fish and "vacuum" them up!

They are giants in every way— even the fin on their back is 4 feet tall!

One whale shark was followed on an incredible journey across the Pacific Ocean. In 37 months it swam 8,078 miles.

MILD-MANNERED MONSTERS
GENTLE GIANTS
OF THE OCEAN

Some giant sharks are described as harmless, but don't be fooled—these fish may not be interested in eating *you*, but they are able to catch and consume vast numbers of small animals. That makes them some of the most successful carnivores of the seas.

Near its surface, ocean water is like a soup—with lots of tiny tidbits floating about. Basking sharks, whale sharks, and megamouths scoop up these tasty creatures rather than hunting their prey. They are called filter feeders because of the unusual way they catch their food.

TWIST IT!

Fewer than 60 megamouths have ever been seen. Nearly all of them were already dead when they were found, which is why we know so little about how they live.

Basking sharks are not usually dangerous, but their rough skin can hurt a diver—and they have been known to attack fishing boats after being harpooned.

Most whale sharks are about 32 feet long, but the largest ever seen was 44 feet—that's about the same as the length of a school bus!

FILTER FACTS

BASKING SHARKS

Basking sharks swim near the surface of the ocean, with their large mouth agape. The shark's mouth can measure up to 3 feet 4 inches wide and contains around 1,500 tiny teeth.

BIG WORD ALERT

BIOLUMINESCENCE

say bio-loo-min-ess-ens
This is light that is made by living things. It is quite common in marine animals.

Ripley's Believe It or Not!®

This diver was nearly sucked up into the mouth of the largest fish in the sea, the whale shark. Despite its size, whale sharks only eat plankton and if the diver had ended up in its mouth, the shark would have just spat him out!

The megamouth is one of the world's most mysterious animals. It was first discovered in 1976, when a male got caught in the anchor ropes of an underwater research vessel. Its vast mouth led to its scientific name Megachasma pelagios, which means "Enormous cave of the sea."

IT'S MEGA!

Megamouths grow up to over 16 feet. They have flabby skin, deep-set eyes, and blunt heads, and are not fast swimmers. They feed on small animals, such as jellyfish and shrimps, which may be attracted to their gaping mouth by bioluminescent spots that surround their fleshy lips.

TOXIC TREATS

NATURE'S SILENT ASSASSINS

Substances that do harm are described as poisonous, or toxic. Every one of the animals here produces a toxic cocktail that can have lethal effects. Read on to find out about some of this planet's most dangerous animals.

Don't be fooled by these beasts. They may not be big but they have toxic power to knock out nerves, destroy muscles, inflict pain, stun, injure, and kill. Sometimes killing with toxins takes a lot out of an animal—check out the gross story about the sea cucumbers to discover exactly what we mean!

PUFFER FISH

In Japan, the flesh of a puffer fish—called fugu—is considered a fine food, but eating it can be very risky. These fish store a deadly toxin in their body, and many people have died from eating fugu. The first symptom of poisoning is a tingling of the lips, followed by feelings of warmth and happiness, but death can occur just six hours later. There is no known cure.

WOOAH!

CROWN OF THORNS

Most starfish have just five arms, but the crown of thorns starfish has up to 20—and each one is covered with poisonous spines. This starfish is doubly-deadly because it devours coral and has destroyed large areas of the Great Barrier Reef in Australia.

22

The bite of a sea snake is painless, but the effects of its venom are not. Sea snakes may be shy but they have one of the most deadly snake venoms. These swimming serpents don't have very big teeth, so they grab hold of their prey and chew, forcing venom into the flesh. Thankfully, sea snakes are very shy and generally stay away from people.

TOXIC TALES

A crown of thorns starfish produces up to 60 million eggs a year.

Starfish make super glue that helps them stick quickly and firmly to rocks. When they want to get up and move about they make anti-glue to dissolve the sticky stuff in a flash.

Scientists think that seaweed contains some toxic treats that can be used to kill the bug that causes malaria—a terrible disease that affects millions of people.

Shellfish such as mussels and oysters feed on tiny toxic marine animals. The toxins can be stored in their flesh, and sometimes get very ill after eating shellfish. that is why people can

TWIST IT!

SEA CUCUMBER

This toxic tale is so bizarre it's hard to believe! When a sea cucumber is scared it forces its insides (entrails) out of its body and separates from them. The entrails expand and split into long sticky threads that attach to the attacker's body. The threads are coated with venom, which target the attacker's muscles, and can cause blindness. The sea cucumber is now safe, but it must survive for months without eating while it grows a new set of insides!

Awesome hair!

SEA SLUG

The color of a sea slug's skin serves as a warning—bright and bold means it's a bad little beastie with terrifying toxins. Known as nudibranchs (say new-dee-branks), these slugs either make their own toxins, or steal some off other animals. Nudibranchs that feed on toxic sea sponges, for example, are able to store the sponges' poisons in their own flesh. Their multi-colored skin warns predators that they contain a toxic treat.

SMASHING GNASHERS

SHARKS HAVE TERRIFYING TEETH!

A shark's top weapon is its mouthful of teeth. Its massive jaws are packed with row after row of slicers, shearers, snappers, and crushers.

Sharks are known as mean, keen, killing machines, but they would be harmless ocean fish without their teeth. A single bite can cut a seal in half, or crush a huge sea turtle. And if a shark breaks a few teeth, it's not a problem—these predators have a scary secret that means they are always ready to kill.

Gross, gruesome, and grisly

This shark is a gut-churning, flesh-gobbling marine monster! Cookiecutter sharks have sucker-like lips and grab hold of their victim with a sucking tongue. The top teeth stab the flesh and hold tight while the bottom teeth carve out a chunk of meat.

Humans have two sets of teeth, but sharks can keep growing new teeth all through their lives. Teeth are arranged in rows, and as teeth fall out, break, or wear out they are replaced. The new teeth grow forward from the rear of the mouth toward the front. Some types of shark may use as many as 20,000 teeth in their lifetime—we get just 52!

Ragged tooth

This shark needs to visit a dentist! His toothy grin gives him the common name of "ragged toothed" shark, but he doesn't care. Those spike-like teeth are perfect for stabbing small prey such as fish, squid, crabs, and prawns.

The serrations (jagged edge) on the side of a shark tooth help it work like a saw, slicing through muscle and bone. Some sharks can even break through the shell of a sea turtle. Shark teeth often have more than one cusp (pointy bit).

Big tooth!

On the left is the tooth of a great white shark and on the right is a tooth from an ancient shark called Megalodon. The Megalodon tooth is bigger than your hand! It was one of the largest fish to ever live.

Swell smile

This big mouth holds about 120 teeth and it belongs to a swell shark. This predator lies on the seabed at night with its mouth wide open, and waits for fish or other animals to be swept in by the currents. If it gets scared, a swell shark grabs its tail with its mouth and swallows water and swells up so it looks bigger than it really is.

KEY FACTS

THE BEST TEETH FOR THE JOB

Sharks need the right teeth for the type of animal they like to catch and eat.

Thick, plate-like, and tough

Great for crushing crabs and other shellfish

Long, narrow, and needle-like

Perfect for holding slippery fish and squid

Big, sharp, cusped, and serrated

Ideal for big meat eaters

SUPERB ASSASSINS

KILLERS WITH SPECIAL SKILLS

Punching, walloping, crushing, and shooting—they are all good ways to stun your victim. Meet some of nature's most creative killers. Some of them look curious, some of them even look cute, but they are all pretty handy when it comes to delivering a death-blow.

Over millions of years, animals have developed crafty ways to protect themselves from attack. Predators have had to change to keep up, in a process called evolution. It has led to the appearance of some astonishing killing skills.

Mantis shrimp

It's thought that mantis shrimps have the best color vision of any animal. Even more impressive, they can deliver a punch with as much force as a bullet! Each wallop is so powerful that it can kill a crab in less than a second, and can even shatter the thick glass of a fish tank.

Orange fiddler crab

This orange fiddler crab likes to show off! One huge claw is half of his whole bodyweight, and painted in flashy colors. He waves it at other males to tell them to stay away, but if they don't take the hint then an "arm-wrestle" might follow.

Pistol shrimp

These little crustaceans can kill their prey while keeping a safe distance. They snap their claws shut with such speed that they fire out bubbles. As the bubbles collapse they reach a very high temperature, producing a flash of light and a cracking sound. This stuns the victim, so the shrimp can move in to eat.

Cone shell

This shelled animal may look as harmless as a garden snail, but looks can be deceptive. The cunning killer can fire a deadly harpoon at its prey. It carries fast-acting deadly venom that disables the victim, which is then pulled under the shell to be devoured.

Eaten alive

The gorgeous patterns on a harlequin shrimp's body tell predators that it is toxic to eat. It gets its poison from the bodies of starfish that it eats. These small shrimps have huge paddle-like legs, which they use to flip a starfish over, so they can reach the soft parts they like the best.

BUTTOM BITERS

Watch out below, there's a shocking surprise lurking on the seabed! Some sharks, and their close cousins rays, hover near the ocean floor to find the tastiest morsels to eat.

Living on the ocean floor requires a different body shape. These fish have flat bodies and are camouflaged, so they can lie still for hours waiting for their victims to come close. When the time is just right, they suddenly lunge forward to grab, bite, and swallow.

BIG WORD ALERT
CAMOUFLAGE
The colors or patterns that help an animal to hide.

What's eating you?

This poor bamboo shark was minding its own business when the ground seemed to open up and swallow it! A tasseled wobbegong shark was the culprit—these sharks are so well camouflaged they are almost invisible until they stir into action.

Wobbegongs belong to a group called the carpet sharks—and it is easy to see why, with their exotic skin patterns. The tassels around the shark's mouth look like seaweed, and really help it to blend in.

KEY FACTS

MEET THE FAMILY

Rays are closely related to sharks, and belong to the same family of fish. Like sharks, their skeletons are made of cartilage not bone.

- ☑ Flat bodies
- ☑ Eyes on the top of their head
- ☑ Fins are like "wings" and they "fly" through water

What's shocked you?

Electric rays have special superpowers. They find their prey by detecting the electricity made in the muscles of other animals. Even more shocking—they can create their own knock-out electrical charge. It is enough to stun animals, or to scare away predators.

Electric rays make a strong electric current in the two kidney-shaped organs near their eyes.

What's stabbing you?

A flick, a twist, and a quick, sharp stab—that's all it takes for a stingray to deliver a nasty toxic blow. These fish have sharp spines on their long tail, which are equipped with venom. Stingrays normally only use their sting to defend themselves.

TWIST IT!

Warriors used to put stingray spines on their spears and daggers.

Doctors in Ancient Rome liked to treat their patients with a quick electric shock from a stingray!

Large Atlantic torpedo rays can generate 220 volts of electricity in one go, but smaller rays can only generate about 40 volts.

IT'S A SHOCKER

Ripley's Believe It or Not!®

Australian TV star Steve Irwin loved animals, but his passion for wildlife led to his death in 2006. He was filming a program called Ocean's Deadliest when a stingray lashed out at him with its venomous tail, piercing Irwin in the chest. Sadly, this freak accident caused the star's death.

VIOLENT VISITORS

HUNGRY HUNTERS
DROP IN FOR A FEAST

Danger overhead!

Ocean hunters don't just lurk on ice, or under the water's dark surface. Some of them attack from above, swooping down from the sky and grabbing wriggly fish in their terrible talons. White-tailed sea eagles can see fish from far away, and dive at speeds of 100 mph.

The ocean is one giant larder—stacked with protein-packed meals for hungry hunters. These predators enjoy a marine-style pick and mix from a tasty collection of fish, squid, seal, and jellyfish.

Not all ocean animals spend their lives underwater. Some of them swim on its surface, spend time on land as well as in the sea, or drop in for food then fly back to the sky above.

I AM THE WALRUS

Sharks are famous for their teeth, but the walrus has got to have some of the most impressive teeth found in the oceans. Both male and female walruses grow tusks up to 3 feet long. Walruses use their teeth to fight and pull themselves out of the water.

BIG WORD ALERT
MAMMAL
Animal with fur or hair that gives birth to live young, and feeds it milk.

Food chains

Big animals eat smaller animals. You can create links between animals that feed on one another to make a food chain. These diagrams show how all the animals and plants in a place need each other. It's called an ecosystem.

Tiny plants

Tiny animals

Bottom of the food chain

Sea bears

Most bears live on land, but polar bears live on the frozen Arctic Ocean, and love snow, ice, and being in the water. In fact, they are amazing swimmers and their scientific name, *Ursus maritimus*, even means sea bear. Polar bears mostly hunt ringed seals. They wait for the seals to pop their head up through holes in the ice then nab them with their massive paws and strong claws.

TWIST IT!

A female scientist in Antarctica was attacked and killed by a leopard seal in 2003. It was the first time one of these brutal beasts is known to have targeted a human.

Fast swimming walruses have been known to attack small boats, and use their tusks to wound those inside.

A sea eagle's eyesight is thought to be six times sharper than a human's.

Polar bears hate being dirty. After eating, they dive in to the sea for a bath and often spend 15 minutes at a time washing the blood off their jaws and paws! If they are too far from water they clean themselves with snow instead.

ATTACK-ATTACK

Mean machines

Leopard seals are regarded as one of the meanest, deadliest, and most dangerous sea mammals. They are massive beasts—up to 10 feet long—with clawed flippers and sharp teeth. They hide in the water, underneath layers of ice, and wait for penguins to dive in—then pounce. They also hunt underwater, chasing squid through cold Antarctic seas.

Fish

Seal

Polar bear

Top of the food chain

HAMMERHEADS

BIG HEADS, SHY SHARKS

There is one way to describe this strange group of big-headed sharks—they're extraordinary! There are eight different types of hammerhead shark, and they look like nothing else on Earth.

Long ago, an ordinary shark gave birth to a shark with a very wide head, and that shark probably became the ancestor of all modern hammerheads. It was a freak of nature, but its big head proved to be a bizarre boost to its hunting skills.

HEAD OF THE FAMILY

The eight different types of hammerhead shark:

* Great hammerhead
* Scalloped
* Smooth
* Smalleye
* Bonnethead
* Scoophead
* Mallethead
* Winghead

GREAT CANNIBALS

The great hammerhead can grow to 20 feet and its enormous size means it can hunt large fish, squid, octopuses, and other hammerheads! Its favorite meal is a stingray, and a hammerhead uses its huge head to pin a ray to the seabed while it begins to munch. Hammerheads are not bothered by a stingray's nasty weapon, and even eat its venomous tail. Hammerheads occasionally attack humans, but they are mostly shy sharks.

Dorsal fin is very tall

Huge head

25 triangular teeth in each jaw

Top tail lobe is bigger than the bottom tail lobe

Eyes on the edge of each "hammer"

Too cool for school

Enormous schools of scalloped sharks gather in the warm waters around to be California, but they don't seem to be doing any learning. In fact, they just swim slowly up and down. They even ignore tasty fish swim by. No one knows why they do much at all. They just swim fish and swim by, but the schools are mostly made up of females. that do this, but the schools are mostly

Why does a hammerhead have a hammer head?

* Its wide head works like two wings. These "wings" have a flat bottom and curved top, like an airplane wing. This shape lifts the hammerhead through the water. The edges of each "wing" work like airplane wing flaps and the shark can change its shape, allowing it to make very sharp turns left or right.

* The hammerhead's organs of sense (for sight, smell, and electrical detection) are spread over a wider area, so the shark can find prey better than other sharks.

* The eyes are on the ends of the "wings." This helps the hammerhead focus well on prey, and it can even work out exactly how close its victim is.

DANCING QUEEN

Female scalloped hammerheads love to dance and they like a clear dance-floor. They shake their head and twist their body in a move called the "shimmy." Then they do a super-fast full spin in the water—that's a "corkscrew." The dancers barge any other shark that gets too close!

GOING GOLD

One type of hammerhead turns bright yellow when it is a teenager! A small number of smalleye hammerheads feed on yellow catfish and golden shrimp, and the color of this food affects the sharks' skin.

DEADLY DOLPHINS

People tend to think of dolphins as cute, adorable, and friendly animals. In fact, they are marine hunters with big appetites, huge brains, jaws packed with rows of teeth, and a killer instinct. Dolphins are part of the whale family.

THESE GUYS ARE DANGEROUS

Echolocation—hunting by sound

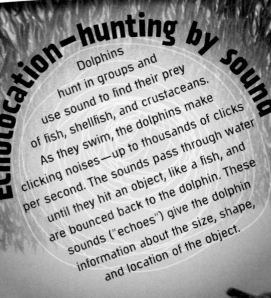

Dolphins hunt in groups and use sound to find their prey of fish, shellfish, and crustaceans. As they swim, the dolphins make clicking noises—up to thousands of clicks per second. The sounds pass through water until they hit an object, like a fish, and are bounced back to the dolphin. These sounds ("echoes") give the dolphin information about the size, shape, and location of the object.

ORCA SLAUGHTER

Orcas love to spend time in groups, which are called pods. When one eagle-eyed orca spies a seal resting on an ice floe, he tells the rest of the gang, and together they hatch a cunning plan to catch it.

2 They create a large wave that washes over the ice.

1 First, several orcas swim together towards the seal.

The largest of all dolphins are orcas and they can grow up to 30 feet long. Orcas are also known as killer whales and they hunt almost anything, from turtles to sharks, seals, and even other dolphins and whales.

TWIST IT!

Shh! It may be a top secret, but there are rumors that dolphins have been trained to help countries during times of war. They have been taught how to find bombs underwater and seek out enemy swimmers.

Orcas sometimes force their way through slabs of ice to reach animals standing there. They can break slabs 3 feet thick!

A dolphin mother and her baby "talked" to each other using telephones hooked up in their separate tanks. Scientists say dolphins chat to each other just like humans!

Orcas are not scared of great white sharks, and attack them from underneath. They often pull sharks out of the water. They often pull sharks out of the water—possibly to stop them from breathing.

KEY FACTS

BRILLIANT BRAINS

Dolphins are super smart animals. These are just a few of the clever things they can do:

✳ Follow instructions given by humans.

✳ Recognize the names for many objects, such as "ball."

✳ Copy human speech.

✳ Answer questions correctly.

NASTY NARWHALS

These dolphins only have one growing tooth, but it is a big one! It grows into a long tusk, up to 10 feet in length, and it is probably used for fighting rather than hunting, as females rarely have them.

3 This often plunges the seal into the water.

Unusually, however, on this occasion the seal catches a lucky break. A nearby huge humpback whale came along and frightened off the hungry orca.

CLOSE ENCOUNTERS

FACE TO FACE WITH SHARKS

The oceans are wide and deep, and millions of sharks live their lives without seeing a human being. Close to shore, however, the story is different—and risky. This is the conflict zone, where two top predators fight for space.

Sharks and people prefer to keep their distance from one another, but sometimes we have to share our habitats. Many people build their homes close to seas and rivers where sharks hunt. While some of those sharks do not pose any danger, some of them make bad neighbors!

Tiger sharks are one of the most feared predators in the world. They are close to great whites in size and ferocity.

BURP!

TWIST IT!

In 2012, a huge shark tank in a Chinese shopping center cracked and exploded. The sharks weren't trying to escape: a drop in temperature and weak construction probably caused the accident.

It is hard for a shark to live in fresh water—their bodies are perfect for salty water. They cope with a fresh water environment by peeing in it, a lot!

SHARK TALES

Tiger sharks often follow big ships, feasting on the waste that is thrown overboard.

LAZY LEMONS

It's thanks to the lazy nature of lemon sharks that we have learned so much about sharks. Lemon sharks have bad eyesight and live in murky, shallow waters around mangrove swamps, reefs, and river mouths. They are not especially dangerous to humans, so scientists and shark-lovers have been able to get close to large groups of them.

They have learned:

* You can turn a lemon shark upside down to make it sleepy.

* When lemon sharks are scared they throw their stomach out of their mouth.

* Lemon sharks are so bendy they can turn and bite anything that is touching their tail.

Diver Eli Martinez from Texas has learned how to play with one of the most dangerous sharks, the tiger shark. He visits Tiger Beach in the Bahamas twice a year to interact with both tiger and lemon sharks, and they are so used to him being around that they roll over under his touch.

THE SWIMMING TRASHCAN!

Tiger sharks, named for their dark stripes, are also known as swimming trashcans. They aren't fussy eaters and will swallow almost anything they find. Here are some of the things that have been found in their stomach. Tiger sharks live in shallow water including river mouths, which means they have plenty of opportunity to eat the stuff that humans have thrown into the sea. Unfortunately, it also means they sometimes come face to face with humans who are washing, fishing, or swimming.

Cats

Ah, poor Tiddles.

Human body parts   Yikes!

Shoes

Woah, cannibal alert!

Sharks

Dogs

We told Fido not to swim too far out...

Birds

TENTACLED

TERRORS

SUPER SUCKERS
AND BITING BEAKS

The deep seas are home to some extraordinary animals, but these scary creatures look like nothing else on Earth. They have big bulging eyes, eight arms, and unusual ways to outsmart their enemies.

Octopuses and squid are the biggest and most intelligent animals without backbones in the world. Along with cuttlefish, they are related to shellfish, slugs, and snails but their amazing lifestyles and big brains set them apart from their relatives.

Crazy creatures

Cuttlefish, squid, and octopuses are bizarre beasts: they have BLUE BLOOD that is pumped by THREE HEARTS. They swim by jet propulsion, and can walk or crawl with tentacles or arms that are covered with powerful suckers. Their toothless mouth is equipped with a tough beak—and some of them are venomous.

Magicians too!

These guys also have special skin, which can change color in the blink of an eye. They are shape-shifters, too, and can transform their body shape as well as the texture of their skin. These are all great ways to hide from predators and prey, but when those tricks don't work they simply disappear in a cloud of dark ink.

Squid and cuttlefish have eight arms and two tentacles. Octopuses have eight arms.

Copy cats

Meet the mimic octopus, the world's most astonishing quick-change artist. It can turn its hand—or tentacles—to creating almost any disguise it fancies. When danger threatens, it can change its color and shape to mimic (copy) other animals, such as flat fish, lion fish, jellyfish, shrimps, and sea snakes. If all that fails, a mimic octopus has a final trick up its sleeve, and dives into a hole in the seafloor where predators can't reach it.

Take a look at this clever octopus mimicking other sea creatures

Just me!

Starfish

Small but deadly

Most blue-ringed octopuses are smaller than your hand, and this one, the greater blue-ringed octopus, is the size of a golf ball, but they pack a lot of deadly venom in their skin and salivary (spit) glands. Some people have died, and many people have come close to death, after being bitten by this creature.

TWIST IT!

There is at least one report of an octopus coming to shore and wrestling with a man.

Humboldt squid are at top of the menu in some parts of the world, but they get their revenge—often delivering nasty bites to divers and fishermen.

Long ago, octopuses and squid ruled the seas—until fish and sharks evolved.

Octopuses have learned how to open screw-top jars to reach food inside. They have mini brains in each of their eight arms.

Paul the Octopus became famous during the 2010 Soccer World Cup when he correctly predicted the winners in eight matches.

One octopus was seen to change color 1,000 times in just seven hours.

TENTACLE ALERT!

Red devils

Humboldt (or you can call them jumbo) squid are known as "red devils" because they flash bright red when they are about to attack. These marine monsters hide in the deep sea during the day, but swim upward at night to catch their prey near the water's surface. Sometimes they hunt in packs of hundreds! They are known as man-eaters and have razor-sharp beaks that can rip through flesh.

Sea snake

Conch shell

Think you are a shark expert yet? Think again—even real shark experts admit they know very little about the way these secretive fish live. The best way to find out more is to swim alongside a shark, and watch everything it does. Fancy getting wet?

Sharks have been around for about 450 million years, but we've only been trying to find out about them for the last hundred. Today's sharks hold many secrets about their links to the past. It will be a long while before anyone can claim to really understand these mysterious fish.

Goblins and giants

Life in the ocean deep, where no light can ever reach, is tough and few animals brave the harsh conditions. It's a lonely place, where creatures wander through pitch-black water, endlessly searching for scraps of food. This is home for goblin sharks, which have odd-shaped heads and soft, flabby bodies (see page 13). Few have ever been seen, so how they live, and what they eat, is still a mystery.

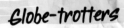
Blue shark

Globe-trotters

Sharks often make incredible trips in search of food and mates. These journeys are called migrations. No one knows for sure how and why some sharks migrate, or even where some sharks disappear to for months at a time.

Blue sharks swim across the Atlantic Ocean when it is time to give birth to their pups, and go on journeys of up to 10,000 miles. They travel for longer and farther than any other sharks. Scientists track them around the world using a simple mapping system that sends messages from the sharks to satellites.

? Can you solve this mystery?

Q. How do blue sharks know where to go?

A. They may be able to sense the Earth's magnetic field and use this to follow migration paths. They probably also use sounds to make a "sound map" of the oceans. It's incredible!

Some sharks lay eggs, but others give birth to live babies, which are called pups. Finding out how sharks find a mate and have their pups is still a big challenge to shark scientists. Sharks are shy creatures, and often go to secret places to lay eggs or give birth.

Shark eggs, however, are a common sight when they get swept up on to beaches. They are like little leathery pillows, and are often called "mermaid's purses." Look closely and you will see the growing pup inside. It can take ten months for a pup to grow to the right size for hatching.

Green giants

Greenland sharks are true giants of the deep, reaching 23 feet in length. They are the only sharks able to live under thick Arctic ice, coming up to shallow waters to hunt. They grow by less than the length of a fingernail every year, which means some Greenland giants may be hundreds of years old.

TWIST IT!

No one knows why sharks don't stop growing, or just how big they can grow to. There may be many more types of shark hiding in the sea, waiting to be discovered.

Some sharks turn cannibal before they are even born—one pup might eat its brothers and sisters while still in its mother's tum!

Scientists always thought that a baby shark would need a mother and a father, but now they know that's not true. A female hammerhead in a shark tank gave birth to one pup, even though there was no male around!

TOP SECRET

Greenland sharks are often blind. They can sniff out rotting food from far away, and are happy to feast on the long-dead bodies of reindeer that have been washed out to sea.

41

A WHALE OF A TIME
NOBLE HUNTERS OF THE DEEP

Oooh, not now, I'm trying to sleep...

King carnivore

Who is the mightiest meat-eater on the planet? Not a crocodile, lion, or even a great white shark—it's a sperm whale. This is the world's largest carnivore (meat-eater), with a massive head that houses the largest brain of any animal. Males need about 2 tons of food every day—and they get most of that by diving to the seafloor and scooping up squid, octopuses, and fish.

Hungry humpbacks

Humpback whales (below) have some neat ways of getting a mouthful of food when passing through a school of fish.

* They whack the school with a fin, and scoop up any stunned fish.

* They slap the water with their tail to create foamy bubbles, which trap their victims.

* They dive down beneath the school then shoot upward, breathing out as they go. Their breath creates a circular curtain of bubbles that traps the school, and as the whale swims through the column of fish they open their mouth and swallow hundreds of fish at a time.

TWIST IT!

Blue whales are the biggest animals ever to have lived. The largest one seen was 110 feet long and weighed the same as 40 Asian elephants.

Whales breathe through blowholes on the top of their head. Humpback whales have two blowholes, but sperm whales have only one.

A sperm whale has no teeth on its upper jaw, and about 52 giant teeth on its long, slender bottom jaw—each one is up to 8 inches tall.

Woah—look at that tongue!

WHALE TALES

Whales are some of the most awesome predators on the planet. They have enormous appetites, and need large quantities of food to fuel their massive muscles and big brains, and to provide power for their incredible ocean journeys.

All whales are mammals, like us, which means they have to breathe air. They have poor eyesight, but find their way through the oceans using a superb sense of hearing, and can talk to each other using songs, clicks, and banging sounds.

Sperm whales can reach extraordinary depths of more than 10,000 feet.

Mini monster-morsels

Some whales eat tiny animals such as baby jellyfish, baby fish, krill, and eggs. This food is called plankton. Krill is especially important for whales—it is a shrimp-like animal and there are billions of them in the ocean.

Humpback whales often lift 90 percent of their body out of the water before twisting and landing on their back—known as breaching. Feeding on a mass of sardines, this humpback surfaced in California surprising photographer Bill Bouton who had been trying to take pictures of birds!

They are able to hold their breath for up to two hours while they swim to the bottom of the sea.

Cooo-eee!

Talking whale!

Beluga whales are also called sea canaries because they are chatterboxes that squeak, whistle, click, hum, and mew. One beluga, called NOC, managed to copy human voices!

F&G 922

IT'S AN OCEAN SOS

SOS is the international code for "help," and right now the world's sharks need our help—and fast. Along with many other super-scary ocean creatures, they face a frightening future.

More than 100 types of shark are at risk of becoming extinct—dying out forever. That includes the most famous shark of all—the great white. Sharks are known as fearless predators, but humans have turned them from hunters to the hunted.

GOING HUNGRY

There is worldwide worry that people are taking too many fish from the sea. It's called overfishing, and it is a growing problem. If humans take too many fish, there are not enough left for ocean predators to eat. That could be why sharks come close to shore—to look for food.

Sharks in the soup

It is hard to believe, but millions of sharks are killed every year for their fins. These body parts are sliced off to be used in soup, which is a very popular dish in some parts of the world. Around 73 million sharks die every year in this way.

Fish food

Many sharks are caught by fishing boats. Sometimes, they are accidentally trapped in fish nets and then die, but they are also caught to be sold as food and souvenirs. Humans kill almost 100 million sharks each year.

Dirty water

Like all ocean animals, sharks suffer when the water is not clean. Humans often pour waste oil, sewage (that's poo!), and chemicals into rivers and the sea. Trash is thrown in too, including old fishing lines and hooks. This is all pollution—and it kills sea life.

BAD

SAFE HAVEN

Some countries are setting aside large areas of sea and turning them into marine parks, where no big boats can pass and no fishing can take place. The parks are safe places where animals can feed and have their young.

A large part of the Great Barrier Reef in Australia is protected by the Great Barrier Reef Marine Park, which helps to limit damaging activities, such as fishing and tourism. The Great Barrier Reef is the world's largest cluster of corals and other exotic marine life.

Telling the truth

When people understand how amazing sharks are, and that they belong in the ocean, they are more likely to leave them there. Teaching people about sharks is a great way to help save them from extinction.

Shark tourists

Lots of people are fascinated by sharks and want to see them. They travel to places, such as South Africa and Bimini in the Bahamas to watch sharks live free in the seas, often from the safety of a cage.

Watch and learn

Animals are happiest in their own homes, but keeping some sharks in large tanks, called aquariums, can be a good way to encourage people to learn more about them.

Studying sharks

Scientists find out more about sharks by using tags. A tag with a tracking device is attached to a shark, and scientists can follow its movements around the ocean. Scientists also watch sharks to find out how they behave.

INDEX

ACKNOWLEDGMENTS

COVER (sp) © Brandon Cole/Naturepl.com,(r) Gavin Bernard/Barcroft Media; **2** (t/l) Phil Yeomans/Rex Features, (b) © Wesley Thornberry - Istock.com; **3** (t/r) © Stanislav Komogorov - iStock.com, (b/r) © Andrew Reid - Fotolia.com; **4** (sp) © Brandon Cole/Naturepl.com, (b) Gavin Bernard/Barcroft Media; **5** (t/l) Pisces Sportfishing Fleet/Rex Features; **6** (b/l) © FtLaudGirl - iStock.com, (b/c/l) © Georgette Douwma/naturepl.com **6–7** (dp) © Doug Perrine/naturepl.com; **7** (b/l) Birgitte Wilms/Minden Pictures/FLPA, (b/c/l) Alexander Safonov, (b/c/r) © Wesley Thornberry - iStock.com, (b/r) © Paul Cowell - Shutterstock.com; **8** (sp) Chris Fallows/apexpredators.com, (b) © Roman Sotola - Fotolia.com (and used throughout); **9** (t/l) © Valerie & Ron Taylor/ardea.com, (t/r) © Willtu - Fotolia.com, (r) © Oceans-Image/ Photoshot; **10** (b/l) Fred Bavendam/Minden Pictures/FLPA, (b/r) Photo Researchers/FLPA, (t/r) © Joe Belanger - Shutterstock.com; **10–11** © tr3gi - Fotolia.com; **11** (t/l) Tom Mchugh/Science Photo Library, (r) Birgitte Wilms/Minden Pictures/FLPA, (b) © FtLaudGirl - iStock.com; **12** (c) © Biosphoto, Jeffrey Rotman/Biosphoto/FLPA, (b) Pisces Sportfishing Fleet/Rex Features; **13** (t/l) © Sea Life Park/ Handout/Reuters/Corbis, (c) Gary Roberts/Rex Features, (b) © Photoshot; **14** (sp) Panda Photo/FLPA, (b) AFP/Getty Images; **15** © Jurgen Freund/naturepl.com, (b) Ian R. MacDonald, FSU (all rights reserved); **16** © Jeff Rotman/naturepl.com; **17** (t/l) © Nicolas.Voisin44 - Shutterstock.com, (t/r) © seapics.com, (b/r) © Shane Gross - Shutterstock.com; **18** (t) © Edwin Giesbers/naturepl.com, (b) © Jurgen Freund/naturepl.com; **19** (b/l) © Kristina Vackova - Shutterstock.com, (b/r) © PictureNature/Photoshot, (c/l) © Ekaterina Pokrovsky - Shutterstock.com, (t/r) © Amanda Nicholls - Shutterstock.com; **20** Reinhard Dirscherl/FLPA; **21** (b/r) © Bruce Rasner/Rotman/ naturepl.com, (t/r) © Alex Mustard/2020vision/naturepl.com, (c) Mauricio Handler/Handlerphoto.com/Solent; **22** (t) © Beth Swanson - Shutterstock.com, (b) © David Fleetham/naturepl.com; **22–23** (c) © Paul Cowell - Shutterstock.com, (bgd) © Gastev Roman - Shutterstock.com, (boxes) © beholdereye - Fotolia.com; (t, b) © Lasse Kristensen - Fotolia.com; **23** (c) © Dr David Wachenfeld/Auscape/ ardea.com, (b/r) © Wesley Thornberry - iStock.com; **24** (l) Bill Curtsinger/National Geographic Stock, (c) Marty Snyderman/Visuals Unlimited, Inc. /Science Photo Library; **24–25** © Doug Perrine/naturepl.com; **25** (r) Flip Nicklin/ Minden Pictures/National Geographic Stock, (t/l) © Jeff Rotman/naturepl.com; **26** (b) © Cuson - Shutterstock.com; **26–27** (c) © Nicolas Aznavour - Shutterstock.com, (dp) © Andrew7726 - Fotolia.com; **27** (b) © littlesam - Shutterstock.com, (r) Phil Yeomans/Rex Features, (c) © Island Effects - iStock.com, (t) © Bruce Coleman/Photoshot; **28** (sp) Tom Mannering/Rex Features, (c) © Jeffrey L. Rotman/Corbis; **29** (t/r) © Visuals Unlimited/naturepl.com, (b/l) Getty Images; **30** (t) © Roy Mangersnes/naturepl.com, (b) © BMJ - Shutterstock.com; **31** (t) © GTW/ imagebroker/Corbis (r) © Doug Allan/naturepl.com; **32** (sp) © Oceans Image/Photoshot; **32–33** (dp) © Oceans-Image/Photoshot; **33** (r) © Seapics.com, (l) Tom Campbell/SplashdownDirect/Rex Features; **34** (sp) Alexander Safonov, (b) © Kathryn Jeffs/naturepl.com; **35** (b/r) © Kathryn Jeffs/naturepl.com, (c) Design Pics Inc/Rex Features; **36** (sp) © Andrew Reid - Fotolia.com; **37** (t) © Photoshot, (t/r) Caters News Agency, (t/l) © Nataliya Kuznetsova - iStock.com, (c/l) © Ivan Bajic - iStock.com, (b/l) © Rich Carey - Shutterstock.com, (c) © Malyugin - Shutterstock.com, (c/r, r) © Eric Isselée - iStock.com, (t/r) © Albo - Fotolia.com, (b/r) © MorePixels - iStock.com; **38** (c) © Georgette Douwma/naturepl.com, (b/l) © Stubblefield Photography - Shutterstock.com, (b/r) © Stephan Kerkhofs -Shutterstock. com; **39** (b/r) © Orlandin - Shutterstock.com, (b/l) © Jeff Rotman/naturepl.com, (r) © Doc White/naturepl.com, (t/r) © FrameAngel - Shutterstock.com, (t/l) Chris Newbert/Minden Pictures/FLPA; **40** (b/l) © Bioraven - Shutterstock.com, (b) © NHPA/Photoshot, (c/r) © Kanate - Shutterstock.com, (c/l) © MichaelJayBerlin - Shutterstock.com, (l) © Optimarc - Shutterstock.com; **40–41** © Netnut43 - Fotolia.com; **41** (t) © seapics.com, (t/r) © Kanate - Shutterstock.com, (b) © NHPA/Photoshot, (t/l, r) © Optimarc - Shutterstock.com; **42** (b) © Brandon Cole/naturepl.com; **42–43** (dp) © NHPA/Photoshot; **43** (b/l) Photo by Bill Bouton, (b/r) © Stanislav Komogorov - iStock.com; **44** (l) © Mark Carwardine/naturepl.com, (sp) © Cheryl-Samantha Owen/naturepl.com, (b/l) © kanate - Shutterstock.com; **45** (b) © Jurgen Freund/naturepl.com, (sp) © Tororo Reaction- Shutterstock.com, (b/l) © Kanate - Shutterstock.com

Key: t = top, b = bottom, c = center, l = left, r = right, sp = single page, dp = double page, bgd = background

All other photos are from Ripley's Entertainment Inc. All other artwork by Rocket Design (East Anglia) Ltd.

Every attempt has been made to acknowledge correctly and contact copyright holders and we apologize in advance for any unintentional errors or omissions, which will be corrected in future editions.